— THE UNTOLD STORY OF —

CHARLOTTA SPEARS BASS

GROUNDBREAKING POLITICIAN

BY NICOLE A. MANSFIELD

CAPSTONE PRESS
a capstone imprint

Published by Capstone Press, an imprint of Capstone
1710 Roe Crest Drive, North Mankato, Minnesota 56003
capstonepub.com

Library of Congress Cataloging-in-Publication Data
Names: Mansfield, Nicole A., author.
Title: The untold story of Charlotta Spears Bass : groundbreaking politician / by Nicole A. Mansfield.
Description: North Mankato, Minnesota : First but Forgotten, [2024] | Series: First but forgotten | Includes bibliographical references and index. | Audience: Ages 8 to 11 | Audience: Grades 4–6 | Summary: "In 2020, Kamala Harris became the first Black and South Asian woman to be elected vice president of the United States. But in 1952, Charlotta Spears Bass was the first Black woman to run for vice president. With key biographical information and related historical events, this Capstone Captivate book uncovers Bass's inspiring story and her historic political achievement"—Provided by publisher.
Identifiers: LCCN 2022051092 (print) | LCCN 2022051093 (ebook) |
  ISBN 9781669016021 (hardcover) | ISBN 9781669015970 (paperback) | ISBN 9781669015987 (pdf) |
  ISBN 9781669016007 (Kindle edition) | ISBN 9781669016014 (epub)
Subjects: LCSH: Bass, Charlotta A., 1880–1969—Juvenile literature. | Vice-presidential candidates—United States—Biography—Juvenile literature. | African American civil rights workers—Biography—Juvenile literature. | African American women social reformers—Biography—Juvenile literature. | Women newspaper editors—United States—Biography—Juvenile literature. | African American newspapers—Biography—Juvenile literature. | Women civil rights workers—United States—Biography—Juvenile literature. | Civil rights workers—United States—Biography—Juvenile literature.
Classification: LCC E185.97.B268 M367 2024 (print) | LCC E185.97.B268 (ebook) | DDC 323/.092 [B]—dc23/eng/20230127
LC record available at https://lccn.loc.gov/2022051092
LC ebook record available at https://lccn.loc.gov/2022051093

Editorial Credits
Editor: Ericka Smith; Designer: Kayla Rossow; Media Researcher: Svetlana Zhurkin; Production Specialist: Katy LaVigne

Image Credits
Alamy: History and Art Collection, 9; Getty Images: Bettmann, 19, Chip Somodevilla, 29, Corbis/USC Libraries/Los Angeles Examiner, 22, dszc, 27, Fotosearch, 16; Library of Congress: 7, 8, 25; Los Angeles Public Library: Herald Examiner Collection, 5, Los Angeles Public Library Legacy Collection/Chas. Z. Bailey, 15, Security Pacific National Bank Collection, 21, Shades of L.A. Collection, cover, 28; Shutterstock: Everett Collection, 13, Julia Khimich (background), cover (right) and throughout, Nadegda Rozova (background), cover (left) and throughout, vectorfusionart, 24; Wikimedia: California Eagle, 11

All internet sites appearing in back matter were available and accurate when this book was sent to press.

Printed and bound in China. 5379

TABLE OF CONTENTS

INTRODUCTION
A Woman Ahead of Her Time 4

CHAPTER ONE
The Early Years. 6

CHAPTER TWO
A Time for Change. 8

CHAPTER THREE
The Power of the Press. 12

CHAPTER FOUR
Becoming a Politician 18

CHAPTER FIVE
A Life of Impact 28

Glossary 30
Read More 31
Internet Sites 31
Index 32
About the Author 32

Words in **bold** are in the glossary.

A WOMAN AHEAD OF HER TIME

Charlotta Spears Bass was a newspaper editor in California with a purpose. She wanted to help Black people gain equal rights and fair treatment, and starting in the early 1900s, she used her voice as an editor to help address **civil rights** issues.

Bass's commitment to civil rights led her to get involved in politics. On March 30, 1952, she became the first Black woman in the United States to become a candidate for vice president. She ran as a candidate for the Progressive Party. She thought it was the only party committed to civil rights.

You've probably heard about Kamala Harris's historic rise to vice president. But Bass's remarkable career as an editor, **activist**, and **politician** helped pave the way for Harris's achievement. This is Bass's story.

FACT Bass ran for vice president more than 60 years before Kamala Harris!

CHAPTER ONE

THE EARLY YEARS

Charlotta Spears Bass was born in Sumter, South Carolina. Her parents were Hiram and Kate Spears. There is no record of her exact date of birth, but it was likely between 1874 and 1888. She was the sixth of 11 children.

In 1894, Bass moved to Providence, Rhode Island. There, she lived with her older brother. She also attended Pembroke College.

Bass began her career with newspapers in Rhode Island too. For 10 years, Bass sold subscriptions and advertisements for the *Providence Watchman*. It was a small, Black-owned newspaper.

The Jim Crow South

In southern states like South Carolina, Jim Crow laws and practices were created in the late 1800s after slavery was abolished. They were intended to sustain inequality between Black and white people. They segregated Black and white people, stripped Black people of political power, and tried to create a sense of inferiority in Black people. Communities created segregated facilities, such as schools, building entrances, and water fountains. Laws made it difficult or impossible for Black people to register to vote. And social relationships such as interracial marriage were outlawed.

A segregated drugstore in Georgia around 1900

CHAPTER TWO

A TIME FOR CHANGE

Bass had asthma and arthritis. They were difficult to manage in Rhode Island's cold, wet climate, so in 1910 she moved to California.

Los Angeles around 1906

After she moved to California, she started working for the *Eagle*. She sold subscriptions to the paper. The *Eagle* was one of the oldest Black newspapers in the U.S. John Neimore was its publisher. The paper was known for highlighting positive news about Black people.

John Neimore

Neimore recognized Bass's contributions to the *Eagle*, and in 1912, an ill Neimore asked her to run the newspaper upon his death. After he passed away, Bass borrowed $50 to buy the paper at auction. She became the first Black woman in the country to own and run a newspaper.

After Bass purchased the paper, she changed its name to the *California Eagle*. She also hired an experienced journalist from Kansas named Joseph Bass as the editor for the paper.

She decided to use the *California Eagle* to cover topics that were important to the Black community, which most papers did not do. At the time, Black people rarely made the news. If they did, it was often because they'd committed a crime, or the papers **ridiculed** them. Bass wanted to cover issues such as housing, jobs, police brutality, and unfair laws instead.

By the 1930s, the *California Eagle* was the most widely circulated Black newspaper on the West Coast. It had a circulation of about 60,000.

FACT Charlotta and Joseph married in 1914 and Charlotta Spears became Charlotta Spears Bass.

PHONE MAIN 1594

The California Eagle

THE PEOPLES FORUM

Volume 29 — Los Angeles, San Diego, San Francisco and Oakland, Cal., April 8, 1916 — Number 9

Watts Citizens Will

March to Victory; Election Monday April 10th

OUR COLORED CLIENTAGE AT WATTS

The colored population at Watts is a creditable one.

In nearly every political campaign since the birth of Watts the colored voters seem to have been able to get together on issues, and have voted solidly. This spirit on the part of our people points towards a solid successful future for those of us who are turning our faces towards this little city of prosperity.

Now it is only hoped that the sturdy, hard working colored citizens of this growing little city will keep their eyes and ears open and keep out those lazy political pirates, who pollute the civic and social life of any city in which they are allowed to operate.

On next Monday avail yourselves of the opportunity of every good citizen—go to the polls and vote this ticket that your own representative citizens published in this paper because they believe, out of their past experience that these men if put in office will deal justly with all men.

Editor J. B. Bass, in company with our San Francisco representative, Mr. H. Shannon, is visiting San Diego and Imperial this week. All along the line Editor Bass is boosting for a bigger and better California for blacks and whites alike.

Seeing the handwriting on the wall, the opponents of Jacob J. Hohn, J. S. Lange and W. I. Hopcraft, are using all kinds of hog wash in their efforts to stem the tide but they have been weighed in the balance and found wanting, and the colored vote which is the balance of power in this election will be a solid phalanx for the people's ticket, headed by Jake Hohn and Jack Lange.

They have stooped but at that will utterly fail to conquer, the old rot about saloon license has spent its bolt and acted as a boomerang. No colored man wants a saloon license. And if he did as long as Watts is wet he would have as much right to have one as any other citizen thereof.

The people are sore and tired of ring rule in Watts and they are all congratulating the colored voters on their firm stand to break it up. The question before the voters is, "Shall the People Rule," and Monday the answer will be echoed back, they will. Hohn, Lange and Hopcraft will win hands down because they are for the people. It is therefore the plain and imperative duty of the colored voters of Watts to stand their ground and in one grand solid phalanx without a dissenting or discordant note, balance the scales in this election for the people.

Monday night meeting of the league was an enthusiastic one and all are on edge for the final fray on next Monday.

THE RAINBOW DRILL AT WASHINGTON HALL WEDNESDAY EVENING UNDER AUSPICES OF MME. C. J. WALKER'S CULTURE CLUB BIG SUCCESS.

Much credit is due Mrs. Vernon Gray and the ladies assisting her for the success of the affair given for the benefit of the Mme. C. J. Walker's Culture Club. The affair, especially the drill, was a brilliant affair, and the twenty-four girl drillers demonstrated thorough and accurate training, much credit for which, we believe, is due Miss Lauretta Butler, who has proven herself master of the art in child training for concert and vaudeville acts.

The character songs by Misses Louise Littlejohn and Green were also well done.

A large appreciative audience was present, and everyone was highly pleased with the affair.

The gentleman and lady holding the lucky card given at the door received presents of scalp treatment on the spot.

PRENTICE DRUG STORE GIVES GRAND OPENING

The opening of the Prentice Drug Store on 12th and Central Ave on last Monday evening was a grand success. People in all walks of life came out in large numbers to pay their respects and to wish the genial proprietor success. This highly creditable institution which will not suffer in comparison with any drug store in the city for its completeness and service is now open for business and solicits your patronage.

Monday evening each visitor was serverd with light refreshments and all left declaring Dr. Prentice the prince of hosts.

NOTED EVANGELIST AND LECTURER WILL SPEAK AT METROPOLITAN BAPTIST CHURCH, PASADENA

Rev. G. W. Reed, evangelist and lecturer, will deliver an address at the Metropolitan Baptist church, Pasadena, Tuesday night, the 11th inst. Rev. Reed is considered one of the best informed public speakers on questions pertaining to the race

He is an orator of no mean ability, witty and humorous. As a story teller he is in a class to himself as was demonstrated in his address at the Forum of Los Angeles some time ago.

He does not allow his audience to go dead on him. He will speak on the subject, "The Truth About a Great Question."

The public is cordially invited to hear this great man. There will be no charge for admission.

WATCH IT GROW

The Sidney P. Dones Realty Company

$75,000 $75,000

I am the confidential agent of the owner of $75,000 and anyone of my race who desires a loan of from $25 to $500, see me at once. The money is loaned at almost one-half what uptown brokers charge. All loans are strictly confidential and private. Open from 8 a.m. to 5 p.m.; from 6 p.m. to 8 p.m.

Suite 4, Booker T. Washington Bldg., 1013½ Central Ave., Tel. Bdwy. 1498.

VICTORY WILL BE THEIRS

Winning Fight by the Independence League at Watts in the Coming Election—Election April 10th

The red hot campaign of Watts is coming to a head and the ticket as published herewith will be elected beyond peradventure, but the Independence League wants to clinch this victory by such a vote that it will forever silence those who stand in the way of progress in Watts. The following is the people's ticket, the men thereon represent the people and are for all the people all the time regardless of race, color or creed. creed.

Trustees

JACOB J. HOHN X

JOHN S. LANGE X

City Clerk

WALTER I. HOPCRAFT X

City Treasurer

SARAH A. SMITH X

Analysis of This Ticket

To say that the above ticket stands for a square deal for everybody is a complete and concrete analysis of the same for it is composed of purely commoners whose honesty and integrity cannot for one moment be questioned.

Jacob H. Hohn

For trustee Jake Hohn as he is called by the entire populace, is a man whom everyone knows. They know that he can have no other than a keen interest for the future prosperity of Watts, as he has large property interests here, he is a plain, common, every-day, unassuming young man whom all may approach and consult on the problems which confront the city and that is what is needed in Watts at this time.

He is receiving the united support of the League and will be a strong winner on the 10th.

John S. Lange

Now John Lange is the one best bet for the people in this election. He has been tried and found to ring true on every proposition which had for its object the interests of the people. As a present member of this board he stands like a stone wall for the people. The people universally hold in the highest esteem Mr. Lange for his great service in their behalf and will give to him a magnificent endorsement on the 1t0h of April.

W. I. Hopcraft for City Clerk

W. I. Hopcraft is one of the splendid citiens of Watts who has since the memory of man runneth not to the contrary, been a booster for Watts. He is out on his merits for this position. The California Eagle desires to give its support to Mr. Hopcraft. He has been a man that has encouraged the enterprise of these people as for many months those who read the Eagle will remember his advertisement was always therein. So for the reason of his fitness and this time because he is with the people against the ring, we urge for him a strong and unanimous support.

Mrs. Sarah A. Smith for Treasurer

Now for this office the present incumbent, Mrs. Sarah A. Smith, has no opposition, but we want to say that she is a splendid, first class citizen and all are proud of her and to know that she has always made good.

DAUGHTER AND FRIEND SURPRISE MOTHER WITH A DOUBLE BIRTHDAY PARTY.

Last Saturday afteronon Mrs. Jessie B. Saunders of Ceres ave. was allured from her home to another part of the city by a friend while her daughter, Mrs. Earnest Jones, transformed their neat little home into a thing of beauty, for lilies, chrysanthemums and green foliage adorned both ceiling and wall, and refreshments toning with the color scheme, pink and white in deceration was brought in.

Not until everything was in ship shape was Mrs. Saunders allowed to return home; and then to be greeted by fourteen ladies, who cried with one accord "Surprise."

As the afternoon died away and evening came on the guests after a very happy reunion dispersed, only, however, to be reimbursed by a new gathering, who came generalled by Mrs. M. Dawson, who was in charge in the evening.

When the guests had been gathered together the big birthday cake loaded with fifty-three delicate little candles was lighted. An excellent program was rendered, Mrs. D. Martin singing, "The Perfect Day," which charmed everyone present.

Mrs. Saunders, who because of her cheery disposition is loved by her friends an neighbors said to The Eagle representative, "My cup is running over with joy and I think it was very sweet of my daughter and Mrs. Dawson to think of this for me."

Mrs. Saunders was the recipient of many beautiful tokens.

CLUB AND SOCIAL DOINGS

Clarence L. James is Host of Progressive Club

Miss Ruth Temple, after spending a week of her vacation with us, has returned to Loma Linda to again take up her studies.

While here, Miss Temple visited the Progressive Literary Club and was much elated at the progress made by them since her last visit.

Miss Josephine Baker gave a splendid concert which was featured with many new hits in the musical world as well as splendid recitations, last Tuesday night, at First Baptist Church, Furlong.

Clarence L. James, superintendent of the Second A. M. E. church, is in Riverside for the S. S. Convention. He expects to remain over until Saturday evening.

Unless some one renders aid to the "Poly Social" Club, we are inclined to believe that they will not last long.

The club made a mistake in not qualifying their membership, and as a result, cannot do anything with some of their members.

They ought to take a peek at what their little sister, The Progressive Club, is doing.

The Sunday afternoon club, of which Lawrence Patterson is president, could also use some advice. The sooner that some of our young people learn that we are not to act as children, but pattern after the older people, the better it will be for us all.

"VENGEANCE IS MINE," SAITH THE LORD

While ministers of the Gospel both white and black are crying from their pulpits "Repent for the kingdom of God is at hand, while sinners are crying "What shall we do to be saved;" and while the 10th Cavalry, a regiment of black men are marching as it were into the very mouth of hell in Mexico—Oklahoma wrestles with eGorgia for honors in the perpetuation of heinous crimes upon the "Black Men" within her borders.

Tuesday, April 4th

(Special to the L. A. Tribune)

IDABEL, Okla., April 3.—Identified by his girl victim as the man who criminally assaulted her, Oscar Martin, colored, was lynched in the court room here today.

Martin was having his preliminary hearing. The girl took the witness stand and identified him. Immediately a number of men quietly arose, disarmed the officers and seized him.

A rope was tied around his neck, fastened to a projection and he was shoved from a platform in the court room. As he dangled there one of the mob shot him twice. The crowd dispersed at once. No arrests were made.

Is it possible that this government, founded upon a constitution that says that all men shall enjoy rights and privileges, will continue to call upon its black soldiers to intervene in the Philippines and Mexico and not protect those same citizens and soldiers from the howling mobs of the Southland, that blight this civilization and cast reflection upon the religion of the age.

Oh, Uncle Sam, we pray thee to bend thy proud head and have mercy upon these thy black subjects for the God whom we give jects for the God whom we serve is not dead, and neither are these black soldiers who stand ready to protect and defend this country asleep to the treatment you administers as compensation for service.

SOME MEETING

There was called to meet at the 14th street school on last Monday evening what was to be a harmony or get together meeting of the Republican voters of the 74th Assembly district. It was the plan to unite the various clubs into one district organization, but there was nothing doing.

We have taken part in many meetings, some stormy ones, in the last quarter of a century but of all the meetings that we have ever attended this one caps the climax. It was some meeting. There was one man walking up and down the floor who defied the whole gathering to make him "sit down;" there was another jumping up every minute or so with a point of order; there was another and divers ones who seemed bent on the idea that HARMONY was just the thing they did not want. This in no way describes the meeting. It was disgusting to good citizens. So raw it was that many arose abruptly and left, especially when a preacher arose and commenced to recite how he loved his people. A funny incident took place as the club man left a preacher who was on the floor said "there goes my friend; he gave me three dollars for my church." Another person close by said, "how much gin?" The question was unanswered. In all fairness to Mr. Utterback, who acted as chairman, let it be said he was fair and impartial and gave to all a fair and square deal. But the wreckers were there to wreck and there was nothing doing, and there never will be as long as these forces are allowed to be recognized in organized bodies.

So the district organizations stand as they were and we suppose will each work in their own way. The regular 74th district club, of which J. H. Penson is the president, will hold a monster rally the date of which will be announced next week.

Samuel O. Bell of hte Torpedo Boat, Perry, stationed at San Diego, was a pleasant visitor to our office this week.

Mr. Bell has been in the U. S. service two years. Before entering the navy he lived in Los Angeles and Pasadena respectively. With a personal glimpse of Mr. Bell we were impressed with him as being a splendid young man with ability as a song writer. Already his "Won't you come out to California and Me" has wide circulation and high appreciation by those persons who have been fortunate enough to secure copies.

Mr. Bell tells us that he has several other songs now in the hands of the publishers.

"Won't you Come Out to California and Me" is light and airy in tone, but filled with a pathetic ring akin to a craving for the aesthetic and beautiful.

We must judge his future efforts by this first splendid production.

AFTER THIRTY YEARS

The editor of The Eagle on his regular business tour at San Diego ran across a cousin whom he had not seen for thirty years in the person of J. G. Bass. Mr. Bass runs the Annex rooming house, opposite the postoffice. We were royally entertained by our cousin and his estimable wife, and spent hours talking over scenes of our childhood days in dear old Missouri. Mr. Bass is employed at the Sanford Hotel and is not only making good there, but as a high class citizen as well.

The Progressive Literary Club held its April business meeting last Saturday evening at the home of Mr. Clarence James.

Plans were launched for the debating and spelling teams. Mr. Agustas Greene and Miss May Rogers were elected captains of the debating and spelling teams, respectively, while Hilbert Rozier was elected manager of both teams.

THE POWER OF THE PRESS

Bass often used *the California Eagle* to battle injustice. In 1915, she spoke out against D.W. Griffith's racist film *The Birth of a Nation*. The film **villainized** Black men. And it depicted the **Ku Klux Klan** as heroes. Bass tried to stop production of the film but didn't succeed.

While the racist film still made it to movie theaters, Bass's **campaign** had reached people across the country. They wanted to hear what she had to say. She began to travel and make speeches. As a result, more people wanted to read her paper, and her popularity grew.

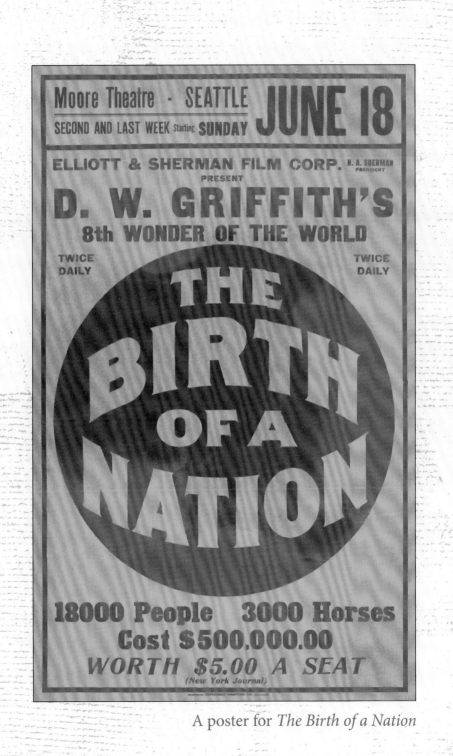

A poster for *The Birth of a Nation*

Bass also used the *California Eagle* to help open doors to employment for Black people. She brought attention to the discriminatory hiring practices of companies such as the Southern California Telephone Company, the Los Angeles Fire Department, and the Los Angeles Transit Company.

In the 1930s, Bass brought the "Don't Spend Where You Can't Work" campaign to Los Angeles. The campaign encouraged Black people to **boycott** businesses that refused to hire Black workers. Her fight against the Southern California Telephone Company was a part of this campaign. In her paper, she encouraged Black Californians to cancel their telephone services and explain that they'd canceled because the company wouldn't hire Black people. After receiving 100 cancellation letters, the company hired its first Black employee.

Black firefighters in Los Angeles in 1925

A sign in a Los Angeles neighborhood showing that it restricts who can live there

In the 1940s, Bass fought against **restrictive covenants** in Los Angeles. These covenants were agreements between homeowners that prevented Black people and other people of color from buying homes in white neighborhoods. In 1945, Bass formed the Home Owners Protective Organization to help fight unfair housing practices. She used her newspaper to inform the public about the limited housing available to Black people. And she helped support a Black family that sued to stay in their home in a white neighborhood.

In 1948, another case challenging restrictive covenants made its way to the United States Supreme Court. The Supreme Court ruled that making covenants to keep a certain race out of neighborhoods was illegal.

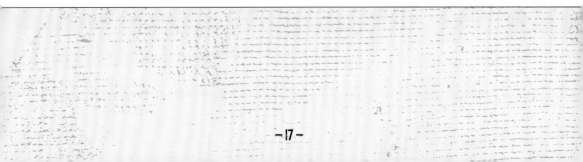

BECOMING A POLITICIAN

When Bass's husband died in 1934, she continued to run the paper without him. She also decided to become more politically active. She wanted to make a bigger impact for Black people.

Bass joined groups like the National Association for the Advancement of Colored People (NAACP), the Universal Negro Improvement Association (UNIA), and the Urban League. As Bass's political activity increased, so did her passion for politics.

In 1940, Bass started to get involved in national politics. She was selected by the Republican Party to serve as the western regional director for Wendell Willkie's presidential campaign.

Willkie campaigning for president in 1940

In 1945, Bass launched her first political campaign. She ran for the Los Angeles City Council. She lost that election. But the loss did not stop her.

A few years later, Bass made a big political move. She helped found the Independent Progressive Party of California. Bass had become frustrated with the Republican Party. She felt it wasn't dedicated to civil rights for Black people and women. The Progressive Party's **platform** did address civil right issues.

In 1950, Bass ran for Congress. She didn't win that election either, but she didn't give up on a political career.

Bass during her campaign for Congress

Vincent Hallinan and Bass in 1952

In 1951, Bass sold the *California Eagle*. Then she focused on her political career. In 1952, she became the first Black woman to be nominated for vice president of the United States. She ran on the Progressive Party ticket with Vincent Hallinan.

Hallinan and Bass's campaign focused on civil rights issues, something Bass had been fighting for in California for a long time. They were supported by well-known civil rights **advocates**, such as W.E.B. Du Bois and Paul Robeson. Their campaign also advocated for women's rights, the end of the Korean War, and a peaceful relationship with the Soviet Union.

FACT The *California Eagle* finally shut down in 1964. At the time, it was one of the oldest Black-owned newspapers in the United States.

Political Parties and the Presidential Election

In the United States, voters pick the next president every four years. Candidates from the two most popular parties in the country—the Democratic Party and the Republican Party—receive the most support from voters. But candidates from smaller parties and **independent** candidates can play an important role in the election. Sometimes, the popularity of their ideas can help shift the platforms of the two major parties.

Bass knew that the odds of winning the election were low. But her campaign was still important. Their slogan was "Win or lose, we win by raising the issues."

Hallinan and Bass did not win the election. Dwight D. Eisenhower and Richard Nixon won that year. Hallinan and Bass only received 135,007 votes in the popular vote. But that put them in third place in an election with eight candidates.

Dwight D. Eisenhower

In the 1960s, Bass retired and moved to the Black resort town Lake Elsinore, California. She also published her memoir. It was titled *Forty Years: Memoirs from the Pages of a Newspaper.* After Bass retired, she continued to serve her community. Bass turned her garage into a reading room. She also used it for voter registration drives.

Bass remained an advocate for civil rights through much of the 1960s. She died on April 12, 1969.

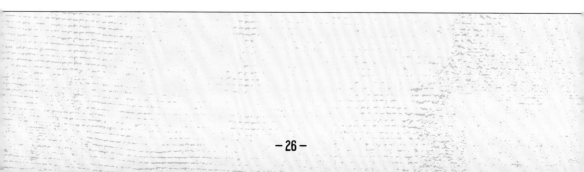

Lake Elsinore, California

A LIFE OF IMPACT

Bass did not become the first Black woman to be vice president of the United States. Kamala Harris would make that mark on history in 2021. But Bass made an important impact as a Black editor, activist, and politician.

Bass dared to do things differently. She ran a newspaper that achieved social change. She brought people together to fight for equal rights. And she brought that passion to national politics. In her own way, Bass helped address many issues that affected Black people and other oppressed groups in the United States.

Kamala Harris

Unlike Bass, Kamala Harris's name is well known in the United States. In 2020, Harris ran with Joe Biden as the vice presidential candidate for the Democratic Party and won. Before that, she was a lawyer in the state of California from 2010 until 2016. And in 2016, she was elected to the U.S. Senate. With her win in 2020, she became the first Black American and the first Indian American to be elected vice president of the United States.

GLOSSARY

activist (AK-tuh-vist)—a person who works for social or political change

advocate (AD-vuh-kuht)—a person who supports an idea or plan

boycott (BOY-kot)—to refuse to buy or use a product or service to protest something believed to be wrong or unfair

campaign (kam-PAYN)—organized actions and events with a specific goal, such as being elected

civil rights (SIV-uhl RYTS)—the rights that all people have to freedom and equal treatment under the law

independent (in-di-PEN-duhnt)—not bound or committed to a political party

Ku Klux Klan (KOO KLUHX KLAN)—a group that promoted hate and commited acts of violence against Black people and other groups

platform (PLAT-form)—a statement of beliefs

politician (pol-uh-TISH-uhn)—a person who is part of, or seeks to be part of, government

restrictive covenant (ri-STRIK-tiv KUHV-uh-nent)—a legal agreement limiting what people can do with property they purchase; some limited who could purchase or live in a home

ridicule (RID-i-kyool)—to make fun of

villainize (VIL-uh-nayz)—to say bad things about

READ MORE

Jones-Radgowski, Jehan. *Kamala Harris.* North Mankato, MN: Capstone, 2023.

Meister, Cari. *Political Parties: A Kid's Guide.* North Mankato, MN: Capstone 2020.

Miller, J.P. *Charlotta Bass.* Vero Beach, FL: Rourke Educational Media, 2022.

INTERNET SITES

Britannica Kids: Charlotta Spears Bass
kids.britannica.com/kids/article/Charlotta-Spears-Bass/633207

National Women's History Museum: Charlotta Spears Bass
womenshistory.org/education-resources/biographies/charlotta-spears-bass

PBS: Charlotta Spears Bass (Unladylike2020)
pbslearningmedia.org/resource/ull20-charlotta-spears-bass-video/unladylike2020

INDEX

Bass, Joseph, 10, 18
Biden, Joe, 29
Birth of a Nation, The, 12–13

California Eagle, 10, 12, 14, 23

Democratic Party, 24, 29
Du Bois, W.E.B., 23

Eagle, 9
Eisenhower, Dwight D., 25

Griffith, D.W., 12

Hallinan, Vincent, 22, 23, 25
Harris, Kamala, 4, 5, 28, 29

Jim Crow laws, 7

Lake Elsinore, California, 26, 27
Los Angeles, California, 8, 14, 15, 16, 17, 20

National Association for the Advancement of Colored People (NAACP), 18
Neimore, John, 9
Nixon, Richard, 25

Progressive Party, 4, 20, 23
Providence, Rhode Island, 6
Providence Watchman, 6

Republican Party, 18, 20, 24
restrictive covenants, 17
Robeson, Paul, 23

Spears, Hiram, 6
Spears, Kate, 6
Sumter, South Carolina, 6

Universal Negro Improvement Association (UNIA), 18
Urban League, 18

Willkie, Wendell, 18, 19

ABOUT THE AUTHOR

Nicole A. Mansfield is an African American author and a mother of three. She is married to her Italian American husband. Between the two of them, they speak four different languages! She has lived in four different countries and 13 different cities around the world! Nicole cares deeply about faith, family, culture, and history. She wants the children of today to learn more about true stories of the past!